Activating Your True Drive Through Effective Human Motivation

By

Juan J. Hughes

Table of contents

Introduction

What is effective human motivation?

A person must be internally motivated. It doesn't matter how you describe motivation—as a need or a drive—because it refers to the internal state when you want improvements in either your surroundings or yourself.

Motivation provides you with the required direction and desire to interact with your surroundings in a problem-solving, open-ended, and adaptable manner once you can access this source of energy.

There are numerous faces of human aspirations, but there are also many faces of motivation. What drives motivation is wanting. People demand changes to their environments, ideas, emotions, behavior, self-relationships, and self-concept.

The essential component of motivation is consistent, enthusiastic conduct focused on your objectives. When you are motivated, you take action and make a move.

The mechanism that begins, directs, and sustains goal-oriented activities is known as true effective human motivation. It is what, for example, motivates you to run the additional mile or helps you lose extra weight. Simply said, motivation pushes you to do actions that move you toward your objectives.

The word "motivation" is widely used in ordinary speech to refer to the reasons behind someone's actions. It is the motivating factor underlying human behavior. The biological, emotional, social, and cognitive variables that drive human action are all included in motivation.

The impetus for behavior is motivation.
Motivation is often classified as either intrinsic or extrinsic. When acting out of intrinsic motivation, a person will do so because they believe it to be right or good. Society's expectations, social groups, and authoritative figures provide extrinsic incentives. As a result, someone may act because they believe it to be right or because they feel pressured by external expectations and situations.

Most decisions need some kind of incentive. People typically don't make significant decisions at random

but rather are affected by a variety of factors. According to the idea of choice, individuals constantly make decisions depending on their internal motives. Therefore, people are accountable for the choices they make.
If this is the case, it seriously affects how issues like addiction are seen. Additionally, it implies that the individual is the only one who can assist himself.

According to research, the behavioral effects of intrinsic and extrinsic human drives vary.
Extrinsic human motivations predict conduct that is the result of conscious thinking and deliberation, such as self-reflective assessments, judgments, and intentional decisions, while intrinsic human motives are associated with spontaneous, uncontrolled behavior and effort-related task performance.

In many facets of life, including parenting and the job, understanding motivation is crucial.
To encourage people and boost your motivation, you could wish to design the ideal objectives and implement the appropriate incentive schemes. Marketing and other areas of industrial psychology require an understanding of motivational factors and how to manipulate them.

Everyone may profit from learning what works and what doesn't in this field where there are several misconceptions.

Set a routine for your behaviors instead of waiting for inspiration or drive to strike.
The distinction between pros and amateurs is this. Professionals make plans and follow them. Amateurs hold off until they are motivated or inspired.

"Making obstacles smaller won't help you get past them; growing yourself will".
-J. C. Maxwell

Results-oriented behavior requires aptitude and drive.

Motivation makes things happen.

Part 1

What are the motives of people?

Exactly why is motivation crucial?

Motivational Styles

Gains from Motivation

Choice Theory

Fundamental Needs of Choice

Social motivations and self-efficacy

Theory of Self-Determination (SDT)

What are the motives of people?

As human beings, it is in our nature to strive, to seek, and to go in a direction of what we want and think is significant.

The biological, emotional, social, and cognitive variables that drive action are all a part of human motivation. The word "motivation" is commonly used in ordinary speech to explain why someone does something; it justifies a call to action. An example would be someone training every day to enter the Football academy while hoping to be a professional player. The desire to play in a professional league serves as the driving force behind intense training.

Every call to action in human motivations must gratify the desired purpose.
It is what motivates you to take action, whether it's starting a diet to lose weight or enrolling in a gym class to stay in shape.
Every motivation has a reason behind it.

The phrase "motivation" refers to elements that initiate, guide, and maintain conduct with a purpose. The needs or desires that underlie conduct and provide an explanation for what we do are known as our motives. Although we don't see a motivation, we may infer that it exists from the conduct we see.

Exactly why is motivation crucial?

Every action a person does is guided by their motivation. Therefore, it is crucial to understand motivation and the variables that may affect it for some reasons.

Understanding motivation may help you achieve your objectives more effectively, motivate you to take action, and encourage you to participate in healthy activities.

Helps you feel more in charge of your life, helps you avoid risk-taking and addiction, and helps you avoid other harmful or maladaptive habits.

We can learn a lot about human nature by understanding motivation. It explains why we make objectives, want success and power, need psychological and sexual closeness, and why we feel strong emotions like fear, rage, and compassion.

Learning about motivation is important because it enables us to comprehend its origins, its causes, what influences it positively and negatively, what factors can be altered and which cannot, as well as the reasons why certain forms of motivation are more advantageous than others.

Human motivation encourages us to achieve desired results like greater performance, improved wellness, personal development, or a feeling of purpose.
It represents something special about each of us. The ability to influence our thoughts, feelings, and behaviors is accomplished via motivation.

Motivational Styles

Motivation refers to the desires or needs that steer conduct in the direction of a goal. In addition to biological incentives, motivations may also come from internal or external sources and be intrinsic or extrinsic (arising from external factors).

The primary motivational styles that are usually mentioned are

1)Extrinsic drive
Derives from sources external to the person and often entails benefits from outside sources, such as medals, cash, accolades, or social recognition.

2) Intrinsic motivation derives internally from the person, like in the case of completing a challenging crossword puzzle only for the satisfaction of doing so.

3)Some study reveals that there is a third sort of drive referred to as familial motivation.
Going to work when you are not intrinsically inspired to do so but are doing it to provide for your family financially is an example of this sort.

Extrinsically driven activities are carried out to get something from others, while intrinsically motivated behaviors are carried out for the feeling of personal fulfillment they offer.

Extrinsic motivation originates from sources outside the person, and intrinsic motivation comes from inside.

In truth, our motivations often come from a combination of inner and external causes, however, the composition of this combination may alter over time-often in ways that seem counter-intuitive.

The proverb "Choose a career you love, and you'll never have to work a day in your life" refers to the idea that if you like what you do for a living, it won't seem like work.

According to some research, intrinsic motivation may not be as susceptible to the effects of extrinsic rewards, and extrinsic rewards like verbal praise may even boost intrinsic motivation.

By taking into account some circumstances, these apparent differences in the researchers' conclusions may be understood. One example is that monetary rewards and verbal rewards like praise may have quite different effects on a person.

Compared to intangible benefits, physical rewards—i.e., money—tend to have greater detrimental consequences on intrinsic motivation (i.e., praise).
Furthermore, a person's anticipation of the extrinsic incentive is very important: Intrinsic

motivation for the work often decreases if the individual anticipates receiving an extrinsic reward. However, if there isn't any such anticipation and the extrinsic incentive is unexpected, the internal desire for the job is more likely to last.

When they feel like they belong and are respected in the classroom, children are more likely to experience the intrinsic drive to study in educational environments.

If students feel that they have some influence over the learning environment and the evaluative components of the classroom are downplayed, this internalization may be facilitated.
Additionally, giving students goals that are difficult but manageable and a justification for participating in different learning activities may increase intrinsic motivation for those tasks.

Gains from Motivation

The ability to change behavior, develop competencies, be creative, set goals, expand interests, make plans, develop talents, and increase engagement all depend on our ability to stay motivated. Applying motivational science to real-world situations enables us to engage students, inspire employees, and coach athletes, children, and clients.

The advantages of motivation are evident in the way we conduct our lives. We need the inspiration to act in the face of shifting situations since we are always adjusting to changes in our surroundings.

The ability to adapt, work effectively, and maintain well-being in the face of a stream of opportunities and threats that are constantly changing is made possible by motivation.

Increased motivation has numerous positive effects on health.

Our physiology and motivation as a psychological state are related. When our motivation is depleted, our functioning and well-being suffer.

According to some studies, when faced with a challenge where we feel powerless to exert control, for instance, we tend to give up easily. Others have demonstrated that we are unable to access our internal motivational resources when we are being coerced.

We can flourish when our motivation is of a high caliber, but we can fail when it is insufficient. Increased motivation has a positive impact on society in many ways, including higher student engagement, happier employees, flourishing institutions, and relationships.

However, unhealthy shifts in motivation also account for addiction, risk-taking, gambling, and excessive internet usage. The motivation that drives addictive behaviors is based on the same brain principles as the complex pleasure cycle and dopamine-focused rewards system.

Because of this, it may be complex and often difficult to alter behavior when there is an addiction.

Curiosity, which is connected to a desire to learn and drives us to learn and explore our environment for answers, can be the source of intrinsic motivation. Because engaging in intrinsic activities results in rewards in and of themselves, they are self-contained.

When we participate in an intrinsic activity, we get an autotelic experience that causes us to focus on the action for its own sake rather than on the results. When an experience is intrinsically satisfying, life is justified in the here and now, independent of any potential rewards in the future.

Activities we engage in for pure pleasure or satisfaction are intrinsically motivated. When we are acting out of intrinsic motivation, we do it because we want to enjoy the action. Unlike conduct that is driven by external factors, it is voluntary.

Human motivations are complicated, and since we are social beings who are ingrained in our surroundings, social groups are frequently significant sources of influence due to the availability of rewards and the awareness of the potential negative effects of our decisions on those around us.

The Self-Determination Theory (SDT) describes how incentives and praise may sometimes have a good impact on motivation, but other times they can have a very negative impact.
Certain reward types have an unintended consequence of undermining intrinsic motivation by lowering a person's sense of competence and autonomy.

When we give rewards, there is a trade-off between gratifying and undermining the need for competence.
Since rewards are used to both control behavior and validate one's level of competence, this type of extrinsic motivation can also undermine our sense of autonomy. With no interference from the sense of autonomy, we want to reward in a way that promotes competence.

Rewards should only be given for uninteresting activities and should come as a surprise. For instance, praise is preferable to cash rewards because it supports psychological needs and has a longer-lasting impact.

As with rewards, it has been discovered that imposed goals limit focus and reduce creativity. Studies have shown that imposed goals reduce cooperation, intrinsic motivation, and creativity while increasing risk-taking and unethical behavior.

The majority of recent research demonstrates that intrinsic motivation is more valuable and effective over the long term. Extrinsic motivation, on the other hand, might be more appropriate in some situations, such as when engaging in boring activities.

It is also possible to make use of incentives more effective by encouraging people to identify with them and integrate them into their sense of self.

Contemporary research on motivation shows that intrinsic motivation that originates from internal motives is often experienced as more immediate and potent than extrinsic motivation.

Today we know that intrinsic motivation impacts the quality of conduct more, such as school work, whereas extrinsic drive increases the quantity of activity more.

It has also been proven that intrinsically driven goal pursuit has stronger long-term benefits because it meets our psychological demands for autonomy and competence, and in turn, produces more positive feelings which strengthen the positive feedback loop and enhance the chance of recurrence.

Choice Theory

The choice theory has been created by American psychiatrist William Glasser. The notion that every conduct is selected as one of this theory's most contentious premises. Therefore, the driving force behind such activity will always be internal. Other theories with a stronger emphasis on extrinsic motivation are referred to as external control psychology by Glasser.
Such psychology, in his opinion, is both incorrect and possibly destructive.

Humans will make decisions based on how they see the quality of the world, and these decisions will be taken into consideration. All of a person's past experiences combine to form this Quality World.
There will be concepts about how to best meet fundamental human needs in this world. Additionally, there will be illustrations of the person's ideal selves and activities. People experience various things as they mature, and as a result, their Quality Worlds will also change.

Fundamental Needs of Choice

According to choice theory, there are five main categories of human needs:

* Things like food, shelter, warmth, and security are necessities for survival.
* The desire to fit in
* The desire for enjoyment
* The demand for energy
* The desire for liberty

Even if the person isn't intellectually completely aware of their fundamental requirements, those needs will nevertheless influence their decisions.

We might also be driven by our need to improve our self-esteem and our want to avoid feeling guilty. Low autonomy and an "I should" and "I have to" language define this kind of behavior self-regulation.

We are considered to have introduced regulation when we put pressure on ourselves out of self-esteem-related considerations and out of fear of failure or embarrassment. Although more successful than outside motivation, this kind of control is nonetheless equivocal and unstable since it is accompanied by internal conflict, stress, and bad feelings.

When we consciously recognize conduct as significant, and when we sincerely desire the result, this generates powerful incentives and leads to identification. When it comes to the maintenance of behaviors involving tasks that are not naturally engaging or rewarding, this more self-determined kind of control is crucial.

When it comes to self-motivation in behavioral change, the balance between control and autonomy orientation might also be important for long-term behavioral change maintenance. People who are autonomy-oriented are often successful in sustaining long-term behavioral changes (such as weight reduction or quitting smoking), but people who are control-oriented typically fail to do so.

The probability of favorable outcomes and approach motivation drive emotional regulation, which is directly related to autonomy causality orientation and preventative focus orientation.

Strong incentives and identification arise when we consciously acknowledge activity as significant and when we sincerely cherish the consequence. When it comes to the maintenance of behaviors involving tasks that are not naturally engaging or rewarding, this more self-determined kind of control is crucial.

Social motivations and self-efficacy

An individual's self-efficacy refers to her confidence in her capacity to execute a task, which may involve having previously completed the same or a comparable activity successfully.

According to Albert Bandura's theory, a person's feeling of self-efficacy is crucial in driving behavior. Our motivation is derived from the expectations we have about the results of our actions, he says, in the end, however, what we do and the objectives we set for the future are determined by our perception of our potential to participate in a certain activity.

For instance, you are more likely to embark on difficult activities and not allow failures to deter you from following the work through to completion if you believe that you are capable of performing at the top level.

Many theorists have concentrated their effort on comprehending social motivations.

They include needs for connection, affiliation, and success among the motivations.

Performance and accomplishment are driven by the demand for success.
The desire for intimacy drives us to look for close, fulfilling relationships, while the urge for affiliation stimulates pleasant interactions with others.

Theory of Self-Determination (SDT)

The creators of self-determination theory are the experts in self-motivation based on the notion that psychological integration is a natural inclination for human progress.
They clarify that while external regulation, such as that provided by incentives, might affect behavior, it does not, in and of itself, create motivation.

Both internal and external variables may serve as motivation for engaging in certain conduct.

Motivation has been the subject of several theories. Theories that are more physiologically based focus on how instincts and the desire to preserve body homeostasis drive behavior. Several theories that concentrate on various social reasons support Bandura's hypothesis that our perception of our effectiveness drives conduct.

A model that illustrates the link between various reasons, ranging from lower-level physiological demands to the very high level of self-actualization, is Abraham Maslow's hierarchy of needs.

We often link a high feeling of motivation with enthusiasm, passion, and inspiration. However, when those sensations go, we are left feeling nervous and looking for them. In the end, we constantly seek some outside stimulation that compels us to act. When it's there, we flourish, and when it's not, we struggle.

The word "defeat" doesn't exactly glide off the tongue easily. It takes time to consider, absorb, and finally have the courage to just spit it out. You eventually run into too many obstacles, at which time "moving ahead" becomes not just difficult but also absurd. As your drive wanes, you're left searching for something greater—a purpose.

Situational motivation directs us toward a certain objective. But the purpose is a global concept. We may rely on it as a strong basis while we are experiencing failure. The lesson of purpose is that we can never be defined by a single experience or failure. While purpose is a way of life, motivation is regional.

Motivation controls our life when defeat overpowers us and emotions rule our behavior. However, the purpose is constant, and it is these few crucial times that we must hold to when inspiration wanes.

Part II

Only you have the power to make life-changing decisions in your life

Why should you make a change in your life?

What drives us to take action, in actuality?

Motivational Elements

Motivational Lack and Depression

Why People Lack Motivation

How Are Self-Efficacy and Motivation Related

The Value of Internal Motivation

How to Form a Habit of Motivation

How to Be Most Motivated

FAQs on effective human motivation

Only you have the power to make life-changing decisions in your life

We can make and maintain changes when we believe we are in control of our conduct. In contrast, people who adopt a victim mindset at the opposite extreme of the spectrum do not.
You have the key to all change.

Simply wanting a change is insufficient; you must also act. Just one step in a lifelong journey, reading this book. Every step must be taken by you since no one else will.

No one will go above and beyond for you besides a few very close family members and friends. Everyone has their own lives, problems, and obligations to attend to, so although they may assist, it is often fairly restricted.
You are the only one who can be counted on to support you throughout your whole life.

Even if someone does offer to help, you still need to accept it. You may have a therapist's support, but you still need to follow their recommendations.

No matter how much attention people are ready to offer you, you are still the most important thing.

In life, an issue seldom resolves itself.
If you are not motivated to tackle your issue, no one will do it for you.
The following is a list of some typical issues and their most probable fixes:

1) You want to give up smoking
Sure solutions include using nicotine patches, reading a book on quitting, and consulting those who have already succeeded.

2) You want to slim down.
Exercising regularly, eating healthily, joining a support group, seeing a nutritionist, and following their advice are some solutions to your goal.

3) You lack sufficient funds
Working harder, spending less, seeing a financial counselor, and following their recommendations are some solutions.

4) Your relationship isn't making you happy.
Changing the dynamic of the partnership, ending the relationship, seeing a relationship therapist, and following their counsel are possible solutions.

5) Your home is filthy
Solutions include hiring a cleaner, making a cleaning schedule, or cleaning the home yourself.

6)Your vehicle has malfunctioned.
Solutions include buying a new automobile, getting the car fixed, or switching to public transportation.

The only need for implementing the almost ideal solutions suggested above is that **you will have to do it yourself.**

The phrases above are meant to emphasize that only you have the power to alter your life. While you may need to enlist the support of other people, you still have to perform the step of asking for or hiring help.

Why should you make a change in your life?

In the end, your chances of transforming yourself and obtaining the life you want are the highest.
Although it is difficult to alter your life, taking charge of the things you can change can increase your chances of achieving your goals.
You only get one, so why not make it the one you want by putting up the effort?

It's not too difficult to learn how to improve your life. The reality of altering your life and yourself, however, is far harder.

Here are 10 actions to take if you want to fully transform your life:

1) Decide to improve your life no matter what.
2) Get comfortable with discomfort by practicing moving outside of your comfort zone.
3) List the aspects of your life that you wish to modify.
4) Specify the changes you wish to make in your life.
5) List every obstacle that can stand in your way of making changes in your life.
6) Pick one important modification or pillar behavior to break.
7) Create a smart objective to keep you on track.
8) Make it easier for your future self to stay with the plan by becoming ready for hardships.
9)Find techniques to deal with challenging individuals and get the support of the people in your life.
10)Have patience, think long-term, and concentrate on the process rather than the outcome.
Last but not least, begin going right away.

No real progress can be accomplished until and until you acknowledge that you alone are responsible for altering your life.

What drives us to take action, in actuality?

Different theories of motivation have been put forward by psychologists, such as the drive theory, instinct theory, and humanism theory. The fact is that many diverse influences steer and drive our motivations.

Theory of Instinctive Motivation:
According to the instinct hypothesis of motivation, permanent and ingrained patterns of behavior called instincts are what drive actions. Psychologists have suggested a variety of fundamental human motivations for conduct. These instincts may include biological ones like fear, cleanliness, and love which are crucial for an organism's existence.

Motivational Theory of Drive
The drive hypothesis of motivation postulates that disruptions of homeostasis lead to the emergence of physiological wants. These demands produce

psychological drive states that influence behavior to fulfill the need and eventually restore equilibrium to the system.

For instance, your blood sugar levels will fall below normal if it has been a while since you last ate. Your body will experience a physiological demand and a related drive condition (hunger) as a result of low blood sugar, which will motivate you to look for and eat food. Eating will satisfy your appetite, and your blood sugar levels will eventually return to normal.

It's interesting to note that the drive theory also highlights the part habits play in the activity we choose to participate in. A pattern of conduct that we participate in regularly is called a habit.

Once we have effectively reduced a drive via a particular activity, we are more likely to repeat it the next time we experience that urge.
Hunger is a consequence of intricate physiological processes that keep the body in a state of homeostasis, which leads to eating.

Your biology is the driving force behind many of your habits, including eating, drinking, and sleeping. Your body needs food, drink, and sleep to function properly. You are therefore inspired to eat, drink, and rest. According to the drive hypothesis, persons have fundamental biological urges that drive their behavior because they must be satisfied.

The Motivational Theory of Arousal:
According to the arousal hypothesis of motivation, individuals are driven to do actions that will keep them at their ideal state of arousal. A person with low arousal requirements may choose to relax by reading a book, while a person with high arousal needs may be inspired to partake in thrilling activities like motorcycle racing.

Levels of arousal are considered possible motivators in extensions of the drive hypothesis. These ideas contend that there is an ideal degree of arousal that we all aim to maintain, as you may remember from your study of learning. When we are not sufficiently stimulated, we feel bored and look for stimulation. However, if we are over-aroused, we will act in ways to calm ourselves down.

According to research, performance often suffers when arousal levels are either very high or extremely low.

However, the ideal degree of arousal is more nuanced than just being in the center of the range. The Yerkes-Dodson law, which states that simple activities are better completed when arousal levels are relatively high and complicated tasks are best completed when arousal levels are lower, describes this link.

Motivational Elements

Additionally, motivation encompasses elements that guide and sustain goal-directed behavior. Even yet, these motivations are seldom plainly visible. As a consequence, we often have to extrapolate from observed behaviors the motivations behind people's actions.

If you've ever set a goal for yourself, such as wanting to change a career or drop 35 pounds, you are undoubtedly already aware of the fact that having the desire to do so is insufficient. Additionally, you must be able to overcome challenges and possess the will to continue despite hardships.

To become and maintain motivation, one has to have these many factors or characteristics. Three significant elements of motivation have been recognized by researchers:

Activation
Persistence
Intensity.

The choice to start behavior is known as activation. Enrolling in psychology classes to acquire your degree is an example of activation.
The continuing pursuit of a goal in the face of challenges is known as persistence. Showing up for your psychology class despite being exhausted after staying up late the night before is an example of tenacity.
The attention and zeal used to pursue a goal are both examples of intensity.

One student can put out little effort (low intensity), while another student diligently reads, engages in-class debates, and takes advantage of chances to study outside of the classroom (greater intensity).
The strength of each of these motivators will determine whether you succeed in reaching your objective.

For instance, if you are highly activated, you are more likely to begin pursuing a goal. If you maintain working toward that objective and how much effort you put into achieving it depends on your persistence and intensity.

Not Being Motivated enough

Various people feel unmotivated in different ways. What impedes certain people may not even be a problem for others. Finding the source of your motivation issues is the first step in overcoming procrastination.

Consider which ones most closely relate to you. Here are six reasons why people lack motivation:

Being too inefficient:
Burnout exists, but it doesn't motivate you to complete them when you have a long list of things to accomplish. You may procrastinate because you feel overburdened by your everyday obligations. It doesn't matter if you work from home and believe you have plenty of time to hustle; just like in the office, sitting on the couch can drain your energy and motivation.

You have doubts:
You don't feel like your finished chores are done correctly when you have self-doubt. To have that feeling of drive to get going might be challenging. To start on the right foot, try telling yourself some encouraging things. Consider the traits and attributes you like most about yourself. Consider how you merit continuing to work toward your objectives, even if it has little to do with employment.

Difficulties with mental health:
A typical sign of depression, anxiety, and other mental health conditions is a lack of drive. As much as you can, engage in self-help and self-care, but you could discover that getting assistance from a professional is more beneficial for your emotions.

Lack of dedication:
Consider how devoted or enthusiastic you are about your task at the moment after taking a step back. Do you agree to do these things out of obligation? You can determine where to add some spice - anything entertaining that provides you motivation and vigor to finish your work - by identifying the tasks on your to-do list that makes you feel less motivated.

Poor attitude:
Even if things don't always turn out as we had intended, you don't have to be stuck in your current situation forever. Negative thoughts prevent you from completing activities and can only hold you captive for a limited time. Even if you're unhappy, a persistently negative attitude will sap your drive until you make an effort to alter it.

Not being sufficiently specific:
Although you may believe that you have precise objectives in mind, are they motivating you? It's crucial to give yourself clear instructions. Vague ideas, without them, will eventually fade. You can't just declare that you want to eat better food. You must be clear about what you want to accomplish and spell out exactly how you plan to do it.

An ongoing lack of motivation might sometimes be linked to a mental health issue like depression. If you have had signs of apathy and depression for more than two weeks, see your doctor.

Motivational Lack and Depression

Lack of motivation often manifests as little to no enthusiasm or energy for activities in your life, even those you would otherwise find enjoyable. While depression also causes you to feel bad about yourself, it also significantly lowers your energy, drive, interest, and attention. To distinguish between the two experiences, it can be useful to ask yourself whether you're depressed or just in a slump. Knowing when to ask for assistance with any disease is crucial.

Although both disorders are associated with decreased energy and enthusiasm for your favorite activities, depression and lack of motivation are two distinct conditions.

Following are some symptoms of motivation loss:

a)Having trouble gathering the energy to do everyday duties
b)Relying on others to organize activities or trips
c)Lack of interest in interacting with or experiencing new or intriguing things
d)Having little or no feelings for either good or unpleasant things
e)Apathetic about your problems
f)A general absence of any feeling around your existence

A few of these symptoms may last for two or more weeks while you're depressed:

a)Almost daily feelings of despair, hopelessness, or emptiness

b)Lack of value and unjustified guilt

c)Weight gain or loss brought on by a discernible change in appetite, either too little or too much sleep

d)Having a restless mood or feeling as if time is passing slowly

e)Experiencing fatigue or low energy

f)Inability to concentrate or think clearly

g)Suicidal ideas

Even though some of these signs may seem little, individuals should seek assistance as soon as they see that their lives are starting to change.

You may become aware of these changes when you struggle to complete your job or schoolwork, when you frequently withdraw from your friends and family, or when you neglect to take care of your fundamental requirements.

Why People Lack Motivation

You should be on the lookout for a few factors that could harm or reduce your motivation. These consist of:

1)One small slip-up or relapse can sap your motivation to keep moving forward if you believe that you must be perfect to achieve your goal or that there is no point in trying.

2)Believing in quick fixes: It's simple to lose motivation if you can't accomplish your objective right away, yet most goals require time to accomplish.

3)Assuming that one approach or method will work for everyone: Just because a strategy or approach works for someone else does not imply that it will work for you. Look for alternatives that will work better for you if you lack the drive to achieve your goals.

Lack of motivation can occur when someone is dealing with life pressures or changes, such as moving away for education, switching jobs, suffering work burnout, losing a loved one, ending a

relationship, getting sick, feeling overwhelmed, or going through other significant life transitions.
A person's lack of motivation could also be made worse by a mental health issue like depression or an adjustment condition.

Some potential causes of your lack of motivation are listed below:

1. Adjustment disorder may be present in you.
People with adjustment disorders tend to lack motivation. These people may be dealing with significant stresses and changes in their lives, but they still struggle to adjust to these changes in their lives to the point where they find it difficult to maintain their routine, daily tasks, activities they enjoy, or engagement with a support system.

2. You Could Be Under Toxic Stress
When someone is under toxic stress, which is a chronic stressor they can't change, they frequently have low motivation. People may feel trapped in this loop, unable to escape their stress, which causes them to continue having low drive. Reduced sleep and self-care can result, which feeds the destructive cycle. People with low or no motivation frequently struggle when they are unable to alter

the stressful circumstance in which they find themselves.

3. You may be experiencing overwhelm.
If you have a lot of duties to finish, especially quickly, you could start to feel overwhelmed.
It is natural to start feeling unmotivated to do any of the chores on your list, particularly if you are unsure of where to start. This vicious cycle can be distressing, especially when worry can sharply rise and feed into indifference.

Breaking each activity down into smaller, more manageable pieces can help you get things done in tiny blocks if you are feeling overburdened. This strategy can assist you in achieving your goals by lowering worry and indifference.

4. You might not Have Many Interesting Activities to Do
You may feel less motivated if there isn't anything to get enthusiastic about or look forward to. As a result, you might discover that you frequently perform mindless chores that you don't find pleasurable, fruitful, or important. Getting out of this rut can be challenging, especially if you are unsure of what will make you happy.

Since research suggests creativity and spontaneity improve inner drive, it can be beneficial to try new hobbies or go back to old ones that used to inspire you or make you happy.10

5. You can be giving a lot of time to others while neglecting your own needs.
You can find yourself lacking motivation if you are continuously working on projects with or for other people and are unable to find time for yourself.

This might make you angry, especially if you care about the folks you're trying to help.
You might not be able to engage in creative activities that would be interesting and further support creative growth because of how little free time you have.

Allowing yourself some alone time each day or every few days to relax and do activities you enjoy will help you feel more motivated once more.

6. You might be exhausted.
Burnout most likely occurs when an individual experiences emotional, cognitive, and physical exhaustion as a result of their employment. Reduced productivity, helplessness or frustration, deteriorated mental and physical health, and

decreased motivation are all possible effects of burnout. A person may be more prone to burnout if they don't feel like they belong in the organization and with their peers.

Burnout may be a complicated and challenging experience, especially if you don't know where to go next. Reaching out to a mental health professional and taking some time to evaluate how fulfilled you are in your current career can both be beneficial.

7. You could find it difficult to shift your perspective.

Sometimes people have inflexible or established viewpoints that make it challenging to consider alternatives to perfection or doing something well. Rumination (worrying), perfectionism, and other undesirable thought habits that prevent the possibility of alternate options for achieving a goal can all be influenced by this viewpoint.

As a result, unhealthy practices that perpetuate the notion that if you can't achieve a goal in a specific way, you can't do it at all, may cause you to feel unmotivated. Challenge the notion or emotion that goes along with the cognitive process and work on being adaptable or flexible in how you can achieve that goal.

8. You might be coping with recent stressful or difficult events.

You might feel upside down or incredibly heavier if you have recently gone through a severe or life-altering event, such as a funeral, the end of a relationship, moving, or leaving a challenging situation. Your inability to manage your new normal may be affecting your motivation in general.

You may be having a hard time processing this experience and don't feel like accomplishing much. In this situation, it may be beneficial to analyze the incident independently and give yourself space to rest and heal.

9. Your goals may be causing you to avoid challenging emotions like frustration or self-doubt.

Consider a challenging assignment, such as writing an essay, and consider the amount of work involved. You might start to feel unfavorable emotions like annoyance or anxiety, and your drive to start or finish this work may be noticeably low.

This could be a result of your discomfort with feeling these emotions and dealing with them while working on this assignment.

You may be more likely to experience immediate avoidance and, in turn, lower motivation if you feel that your level of frustration or self-doubt is difficult to control for the task.

You might even be aware of how crucial it is to complete the task, which would only serve to exacerbate your negative feelings about it not being done.

To improve the sensation of accomplishment when completing work, it might be good to divide it into manageable periods and even reward yourself along the way.

10. You Could Be Going Through a Depressive Episode

Low motivation is a common symptom of a major depressive episode or disorder, even though it can be influenced by a variety of factors.

This typically manifests with difficulty in other areas in addition to motivation (such as feeling sad or hopeless, changes in weight and energy levels), which can make it difficult for you to meet your goals and manage your emotions.

Contacting a mental health professional can be very beneficial so that you can receive a diagnosis and start to understand what is taking place.

How Are Self-Efficacy and Motivation Related

According to leading researchers in the field of self-motivational psychology, there are three ways to tell if you (or someone in your life) is self-motivated:

Can you manage it?
Will it work?
Does it merit it?

You are probably self-motivated if you replied "yes" to each query.

You have self-efficacy if you think you can succeed. If you have response efficacy, which is the conviction that the action you are taking will produce the desired result, then it will work. If you conclude it is worthwhile, you have assessed the benefits vs the drawbacks and come to the conclusion that the benefits outweigh the drawbacks.

Four factors that support self-motivation:
1) Outcomes: To be self-motivated, you must genuinely desire the results of your activities rather than only acting to avoid unfavorable consequences;
2) Competence: If you can affirm "yes" to all three of the aforementioned questions, you will feel competent in your capacity to complete tasks;
3)Decision: Having control over your actions promotes self-motivation;
4) Community: Believing in yourself and your ability to succeed depends on having social support and connections with others.

A psychologist and expert in self-efficacy claims that making self-satisfaction contingent on a certain level of performance creates self-inducements for people to continue working hard until their performances meet internal standards. Both the anticipated satisfactions for matching attainments and the dissatisfactions with insufficient ones provide incentives for self-directed actions.

You will be motivated to meet the internal criteria you set for yourself if you believe you can accomplish it, that it will work, and that it is worthwhile.

The Value of Internal Motivation

While pleasing others and reaching external standards can undoubtedly inspire us to get things done, such efforts aren't exactly labors of love, therefore self-motivation is an important idea.

To put it another way, while many times performing something out of obligation or for an external reward is sufficient, it lacks the passion necessary to inspire creativity and brilliance.

While using external motivation is acceptable in some circumstances, it is less likely to leave you feeling personally fulfilled and to have found deeper significance in your life.

Self-motivation not only leads to higher quality work overall, but it also makes it easier to handle stress and makes us generally happier to accomplish what we enjoy.

Repeating positive affirmations can only get you so far; now that you know what can lead to a lack of motivation, you need to discover strategies to start recovering your motivation.

Try to pick out at least one of the following suggestions that you can begin using:

1)Listen to podcasts that present inspiring, uplifting tales.
2)Be in the company of people who are pursuing their objectives and who are willing to discuss their successes and setbacks with you.
3)As you complete tasks, reward yourself with incentives.
4)Make sure to do something enjoyable for every unpleasant chore you complete.
5)Dividing your to-do list into digestible chunks will help.
6)Incorporate your chores into your everyday routine as habits.
7)Take a stroll outside to relax your mind.
8)Be sympathetic and gentle to yourself.
9)When you think negatively, argue the opposite.

Self-motivation is fueled by a set of abilities that you have control over.

Six key abilities serve as the cornerstone of self-motivation, and you can all acquire them with consistent practice:
1)Establishing ambitious but practical goals (such as smart goals)
2)Assuming the proper amount of risk
3)Seeking feedback constantly to determine how to get better
4)Being dedicated to one's goals, whether personal or corporate and going above and beyond to attain them;
5)Actively looking for possibilities, and when they do, grabbing them;
6)Being able to handle failures and persist in your aims despite difficulties (i.e., resilience).

Additionally, there are six things you can do to keep your motivation high:

1)Continue learning and gaining information (i.e., cultivate a passion for learning);
2)Spend time with those who are driven, enthused, and encouraging;
3)Develop a positive outlook and increase your optimism and resilience;

4)Identify your assets and areas for improvement;
5)Avoid putting things off and improve your time management;
6)Get aid when you need it, and be willing to help others succeed.

Fortunately, there are many things that teachers, parents, and other adult mentors can do to help students become self-motivated, as well as a variety of tactics that students can use on their own.

Here are some suggestions for inspiring pupils' self-motivation:

1)Give students as much freedom and autonomy as you can (for instance, let them choose their seating arrangement or from a variety of possibilities for their final project, and use problem-based learning)

2)Use phrases like "and" and "what if" rather than "but" to offer critical criticism, commend the effort, and valuable feedback to foster student competence

3)Develop a strong bond with your pupils by showing an interest in them, being approachable,

remaining adaptable, having the end objective of learning front and center, and never giving up on them
4)Encourage your pupils to consider, describe, and debate how the material they are learning applies to their own life.

Here are some additional strategies students can use to increase their self-motivation:

1)Give your study purpose and assume personal responsibility for your learning
2)Plan by scheduling your semester, month, week, and even day
3)Create a routine and use time management techniques to increase organization and productivity
4)Identify a few relaxing spaces for studying (they ought to be peaceful and distraction-free)
5)To keep healthy, get adequate sleep, eat well, and exercise frequently
6)"Time monsters" such as the internet, video games, or idle time spent with friends must be tamed
7)Avoid multitasking by concentrating all of your attention on one subject or task at a time

8)Take well-deserved breaks to keep motivated and rejuvenated
9)Establish a network of friends and family who will motivate you to succeed
10)Positive self-talk is encouraged.

From research on the psychology of effective self-motivation, it was deduced that:

i)Self-control and internal motivation
Although self-discipline and self-motivation are two separate ideas, maintaining self-motivation requires self-discipline. To achieve your goals, you must combine self-motivation with self-discipline. Being self-motivated alone is insufficient.

Even though they are all attending voluntary courses with the intention of learning, a study of online students revealed that those who exhibited self-discipline were the most likely to succeed.

High self-disciplined students demonstrated greater competency at the course's conclusion, completed more outside assignments, and were more successful in reaching their objectives.

ii)Motivation for Losing Weight

Self-motivation is frequently a crucial element in weight loss. The two have a definite connection, according to research.

Researchers discovered that participants in several trials who reported higher levels of autonomy support and self-determined motivation were more successful at losing weight, more likely to keep the weight off for longer periods, and more upbeat about their weight loss journey.

We are considerably more likely to succeed when we have our own deeply held motivations for wanting to lose weight, motivations that are focused on personal fulfillment rather than fulfilling external norms.

How to Form a Habit of Motivation

You may create better routines and develop motivational habits by following three easy steps.

Step 1:

A solid pre-game ritual should start by being so simple that you can't refuse it. You shouldn't require encouragement to begin your pre-game ritual.

Starting a task is always the most crucial step. If you struggle to find motivation at first, you'll discover that it frequently appears once you've begun. Your pre-game ritual must be relatively simple to begin for this reason.

Step 2:
Your routine ought to motivate you to advance toward the result.
Physical inactivity is frequently associated with a lack of mental motivation. Imagine how you would feel physically when you were bored, depressed, or unmotivated. You aren't moving all that much. Perhaps you're curled up on the couch, fading away like a bulb.

The inverse is also accurate. It is much more probable that you will feel cognitively engaged and invigorated if you are physically active and involved.
Your regimen should gradually increase the amount of physical activity while still being as simple to begin as possible. Your drive and thoughts will follow your bodily actions. It's important to remember that physical activity need not equate to exercise.

Step 3:
You must always adhere to the same routine.
Your pre-game routine should be designed to include a sequence of actions that you always take before performing a certain assignment. Your pre-game ritual instructs your mind.
Over time, this pattern becomes so closely linked to your performance that just carrying out the routine causes you to enter a state of performance readiness.

You just need to get started with your routine; you don't need to know how to acquire motivation.
Even when you are not motivated to perform it, your pre-game ritual serves as the trigger to start your habit.

This is crucial because it's frequently too difficult to decide what to do next when you lack motivation. You frequently choose to give up when given the option to make another choice. But the pre-game ritual takes care of that issue because you are fully aware of what to do next. There is no deliberating or choosing. It's irrelevant if you lack motivation. Simply stick to the design.

How to Be Most Motivated

Some people refer to this wonderful confluence of joy and peak performance as flow. Flow is the mental state you experience when you are so concentrated on the work at hand that the rest of the world fades away, and it is what athletes and performers experience when they are "in the zone."

In many ways, the state of flow could be compared to your highest level of motivation. It would be difficult to find a situation where you are more motivated to keep working on the task at hand.

FAQs on effective human motivation

1) Why is having a tough job important for feeling motivated?
You won't have something new to strive towards without obstacles. If all of your jobs are simple, you won't be motivated to perform better. Adding challenges regularly might inspire you to expand your knowledge, hone your abilities, and try new things.

2)What factors influence my motivation?
Plenty of elements can affect your motivation. Your motivation levels are influenced by the

environment, those around you, how hungry you are, and more. Although it can be difficult to identify what affects you the most, doing so can help you get back on track. Consider your surroundings the next time you lack drive.

3)How can I assist someone who lacks motivation?
One of the nicest things you can do for someone lacking motivation is to help them when and how they need you. If they're battling a mental illness, you might advise them to get help from a specialist. You can also do that if they require someone to hold them responsible for their everyday obligations. Each person has various needs, so be there for them in the ways that work best for them.

Lack of motivation with ineffective ideas and approaches may be incredibly unpleasant, especially when it prevents you from achieving your goals and developing your personality.

Procrastination is frequently linked to a lack of ambition. You never feel the need to accomplish what you ought to do, which would cause you to overlook any motivation.

Here are a few ways to stay motivated to stay on the correct track:

Find your desire, first.
You can utilize your drive to get better to motivate yourself more. Imagine all the advantages and benefits that come from your daily efforts. You may experience a surprising increase in motivation if you use your drive for success as a method of motivation.

Refuse to be depressed.
To make sure that you are always in a good mood, you must do everything in your power to eliminate your bad emotions. To feel better, you can watch comedic videos or movies. Out of all the motivational techniques, laughing is also a powerful instrument that can reduce procrastination and increase your incentive.

Find your area of interest.
Can you still recall how much you detested math in elementary school and struggled to find the motivation to learn it? Your lack of interest in the topic was the cause of your lack of desire and motivation. If a task isn't enjoyable, just consider the benefits you'll enjoy once you've accomplished the bigger objective.

Energize yourself.
Likely, you won't be able to find any inspiration if you're physically depressed and exhausted. Such fatigue is frequently brought on by a diet high in sugar, fat, and alcohol. Sleep deprivation is another factor. Only you can identify the causes of this lack of energy and implement the necessary changes to increase it.

Divide your aims.
If you break down your bigger goals into smaller ones that you can achieve one step at a time, you can quickly increase your motivation. Once you use these motivational strategies to accomplish one subgoal after another until you attain your main goal, you'll notice a spike in motivation right away.

Your motivation is everything. It's time for you to start motivating yourself now that you understand what it is and how to do it.

People frequently claim that inspiration doesn't last, as Zig Ziglar once said. "Well, bathing doesn't either. That is why we advocate it every day."

It's common to misunderstand motivation. You don't get instructions from a mentor. You are not being forced to practice by a coach.

Motivation is a narcissistic, personal mindset. The person standing next to you is unimportant to it. It doesn't give a damn about what you ought to be doing or what your spouse, parents, or other loved ones advise. What you want is what matters. In the end, you won't be driven if you don't truly want it.

Other motivational techniques that can help you persevere are as follows:

1. Agree with yourself.
2. Fake it until you make it.
3. Starting your day with optimism.
4. Making significant objectives.
5. Always begin with the most difficult task.
6. Have no fear of failing.

Finding strategies to maximize your motivation is the goal of the above motivational techniques. Your potential can be maximized when your motivation is at its highest. Procrastination is eliminated, progress is made, and motivation is demonstrated in this way.

Part III

Taking charge of your life

How to locate and activate your motivation

Guidelines for Increasing Motivation

How Therapy Can Aid in Motivating People

Finding your superpower

Use your superpowers

No one owes you anything, but you owe yourself everything.

The Best Ways to Motivate Others and Yourself

Techniques for Motivation

Self-motivation strategies

Ways to Motivate Yourself Effortlessly

Taking charge of your life

It can be difficult to accept responsibility for your thoughts, deeds, and life. It necessitates a readiness to take responsibility for your actions, admit your accomplishments and shortcomings, and quit blaming others for your predicament.

But taking charge of your life also develops self-respect, grit, and character. It enables you to actively design a happy, purposeful, and healthy life in which you make decisions about how to react to your surroundings in a responsible and resilient manner. When we become aware of the quality of our lives, it affects our outlook, priorities, and behavior. We are free to decide how to respond.

Take charge of your life by owning your choices, being willing to fail, and acting as the change you want to see in the world.

Assuming complete responsibility for what occurs is taking ownership. It implies that your effort is the only factor in the achievement of any result. Because you are alone and responsible for your actions, you are organically motivated to perform because you have nowhere else to turn.

Specifically in terms of personal development, taking responsibility is a must. Because you are working on yourself alone and for yourself, the process is very personal and is made more efficient by adopting an ownership mentality.

This is why it is termed personal development. Sure, it's still beneficial to want to become in shape for your spouse or read more at night to work more efficiently, but the desire to do better remains within you. And that's crucial because when it's the case, we accomplish more.

Work that reflects our distinct talents inspires us and gives us additional passion. With nowhere to run, we realize that the activities we take to get the results we desire are directly tied to those outcomes. We are also much more motivated to avoid failure than we are to succeed. As a result, we go above and beyond and take whatever measures are necessary to achieve more. We are all the biggest fans of ourselves, after all!

So, take charge of your personal growth. Because that is how you get results, do it for yourself and pursue it relentlessly.

People start taking action to solve their problems once they stop making excuses, stop blaming others, and take responsibility for everything in their lives.
Don't hold people responsible for your emotions or your life's events. There aren't many kind people around, but it's your job to force yourself to consider your options and respond appropriately when necessary.

This does not imply that you are to blame for everything that occurs to you. It is your responsibility to be transparent about the boundaries you have set for others. It involves asking yourself, "What can I do to improve? "The others are foolish," as opposed to "the others are stupid."

Take ownership of your actions.
Take ownership of your behavior.
Be responsible for your performance.
Accept responsibility for your errors.

Nobody is flawless, hence it is acceptable to "fail," to make mistakes, etc. And the only way to "fail" and make mistakes is to learn from them and improve. So, rather than saying "oh, I can't do this," say "okay, what can I do better next time, and how can I repair this now" if it happens again. Move past the error and accept it.

We must keep in mind that we are only accountable for our emotional responses and not for those of others. Our natural tendency is to point the finger at others when we have a negative emotional reaction to someone else.

Although it can appear that the other person was the one who "caused" your emotional response, in reality, your reaction is the result of a preconditioned sensitivity to particular stimuli. Certain situations set you off. It is most obvious when you are angered by someone else's actions while other people in the room are not bothered by it.

During your formative years, you become emotionally sensitive in numerous ways. In this approach, particular mental habits are ingrained. The first stage is accepting responsibility for your deeds.

You only realize how strong you are when you accept responsibility for your life.

It can be difficult to accept responsibility for your thoughts, deeds, and life. It necessitates a readiness to take responsibility for your actions, admit your accomplishments and shortcomings, and quit blaming others for your predicament.

How to begin developing personal ownership of your life is provided below:

1. Observe Your Propensity to Blame

Our temptation to place the blame for our predicament on others is frequently a reflex behavior. Therefore, recognizing this initial reaction and the role we played in the circumstance is the first step toward taking ownership of the building. The next time anything goes wrong or a bad circumstance occurs, stop and consider your part in it by asking yourself, "What is my position in this? ”

Similar to this, our propensity to grumble is frequently an instinctual reaction. Additionally, it reinforces a victim attitude and is reactive and passive. If you catch yourself grumbling, take a moment to reflect and think, "What can I learn from this? What is the broader perspective? ”

Humans are brilliant at coming up with original solutions when we need them. After all, inventions are born out of necessity. Therefore, no matter what the barriers are, if something is important to you, whether it be your health, fitness, love, profession, education, or happiness, you will find a way.

Therefore, the next time you encounter a difficult scenario, consider flipping the self-talk by asking yourself, "How can I?" as opposed to adopting a defeatist attitude and eliminating your possibilities by stating,
"I can't."

List all potential solutions to your difficult issue as a great activity to assist with this mentality shift. Allow yourself to write down bizarre and illogical ideas while letting go of logic. It's not necessary to find the ideal solution right away. Instead, brainstorming can encourage original thought, problem-solving, the creation of a plan of action, and a sense of control over the results.

2. Practice Making Decisions

We frequently remark, "I don't have a choice," when we lack ownership, yet we always have a choice - even when we don't actively pick, we're still choosing by default. By being aware of our options, we instill a feeling of individual accountability and foster deliberate decision-making.

For instance, after a hard day, you might tell yourself that you are too exhausted to go to the gym. By saying those words aloud, your gut will tell you whether they are a true, responsible reason — or whether you are blaming outside events via an excuse. Try re-framing that phrase to reflect your active choice, such as "I choose not to go to the gym tonight."

To develop a sense of ownership for your day-to-day choices, start using intentional language:
Your internal locus of control will develop with the aid of this supportive reinforcement of decision.

3. Become Responsive

You are more likely to accept responsibility for your conduct when you hold yourself accountable to others. It will consequently increase your sense of personal accountability. Being accountable to others can help you avoid reverting to old behavior patterns, which can offer additional support when things get tough.

4. Attempt Uncomfort

If you always blame outside factors, you'll never have to venture outside your comfort zone. Although they may feel secure, comfort zones are where change never occurs. Stepping outside our comfort zones and developing a feeling of accountability for our actions are necessary for us to learn, evolve, and create a fulfilling existence.

We are likely to experience some failure the first few times we try something new, just like any newbie. And that's all right. Failure is nothing to be afraid of; it is one of the best methods to learn and shows clearly that you have some control over your results. Making progress requires failing, picking yourself up, and practicing. They aid in gap detection, plan creation, and forward motion.

Always strive for the principle of progress rather than perfection. Making mistakes, learning from them, and making lasting (imperfect) progress all contribute to the development of a sense of direction, control, and accountability.

It's time to assume control over your life!

How to locate and activate your motivation

Even under the best of circumstances, maintaining motivation may be challenging. Even the most tenacious individual occasionally loses their enthusiasm. We could frequently catch ourselves putting things off for no apparent reason. Upon reflection, we conclude that lack of motivation is frequently the cause of procrastination. When you lack motivation, you are more inclined to waste time and give up on your personal and professional objectives.

Finding the motivation to complete your goal is the next stage once you've decided what you want to do. Here are some pointers to help you become and remain motivated.

Identify an objective.

Knowing what one is aiming for to attain it is crucial. So, start by establishing goals for yourself. Make sure your objective is time-bound, explicit, attainable, measurable, and reasonable. Also, make a list of the reasons why and ways to accomplish this goal that are essential to you. Motivation in and of itself comes from knowing what you want and how to get it.

Consider the outcome and your feelings once you attain it. Regularly review your list and, if necessary, make modifications. Just take a minute, sit back, and remind yourself of your original motivation for choosing this path if you start to get lost along the way.

If you fail to achieve your unreasonable expectations, you might become discouraged. Therefore, setting reasonable timelines and goals is essential. However, this does not preclude you from testing your limits. You should without a doubt! It's not a goal if you don't push yourself, is it?

Create an action plan.
Our fast-paced, distracted manner of life makes it simple to get sidetracked and blown off course. Having a strategy in place ensures that you stay on course and diligently pursue your objective. It offers a great deal of clarity and acts as your guide even when things are at their worst. Create checkpoints as well to monitor your progress.

Be reliable and well-organized. For each action you take, have a plan. However, be ready to deviate from your plan if you come into a few minor hiccups along the way. Create a To-Do list and post it on the wall with due dates. This will guarantee that you do your work on schedule.

Give to yourself.

Receiving a reward is always enjoyable, regardless of age. This is a fantastic method to stay going and positively motivate yourself. The reward you should give yourself is whatever motivates you to continue.

Simple rewards like an ice cream scoop after a week of dieting or a late-night movie marathon after days of studying could be used as incentives.

Have you put in a lot of effort this entire month? It could be time to go shopping or treat yourself to a massage. Take a vacation as soon as you complete any significant tasks (such as passing an aptitude test or something like that). You must be exhausted, so take advantage of this time to unwind and recharge.

Take things slowly

Can you consume a whole hamburger at once? Right, no? But if you eat a burger piece by piece, you can finish it. Try to accomplish your goal similarly by breaking it down into smaller steps. Starting small will aid in your progress. As you become more confident following your action plan, you can advance and take bigger actions in the future. Each task's sense of completion should serve as a powerful motivator in and of itself. Your objective will appear much more doable and far less overwhelming as a result of all of this.

Look after your health

Maintaining both your physical and emotional wellness is important. Exercise helps avoid depression and low self-esteem, two obstacles to self-motivation. Move that body, then. Even brief physical activity elevates your mood and makes you feel more vibrant and lively.

Please remember to eat nutritious foods and to eat your meals on time. Even though junk food might be quite alluring, it isn't always healthy for you. Additionally, get enough rest. Rest both your body and mind.

Avoid negativity and justifications.

Keep in mind that while excuses will always be available to you, opportunities won't. So don't put it off!

Making excuses is not being motivated. Try not to allow anything to hinder you from achieving your objectives. Remove the harmful elements. For those trying to achieve their goals, negative thinking is a common roadblock. Therefore, if you begin to believe that you cannot accomplish your goal, the likelihood that you will not increase. So, think optimistically and be an optimist.

Find your distractions and get rid of them. Hold yourself accountable in both your own and other people's eyes. Giving trusted people advance notice of your plans could be the motivating factor for some. They would do all in their power to avoid looking foolish for not carrying out the plan properly.

Seek out assistance
Inspiration is contagious. Try to surround yourself with motivated people who share your goals and who are also like-minded. Your friends and family will be your biggest supporters and will help you get through this trip, so let them know what your aim is.
Contact a counselor who can help you and provide fresh inspiration to keep working hard.

So, if you want to accomplish your goal, being motivated is crucial. Do keep these suggestions in mind, and never lose faith in your abilities!

How can you get the motivation going?

The good news is that–contrary to popular belief–self-motivation can be adjusted. It is not some innate quality bestowed by God. There are tested methods for developing self-motivation, even when things are difficult, according to research.

Staying motivated is difficult since it's not natural. To ensure we continue on the right track, we need to be deliberate with our actions.

Unfortunately, when it comes to motivation, individuals frequently go in the wrong way.

They naively associate drive with enormous, impossible goals and expend all of their energy trying to push through and complete them. In actuality, this strategy causes willpower to weaken and burnout.

Instead, make it challenging and specific from the first.

The American Psychological Association claims that persons who establish demanding and precise goals are 90% more likely to succeed in achieving them.

Our motivation wanes when we create broad, unspecific goals since there are no achievable, measurable checkpoints along the route.

For both your success and the morale and motivation of your team, it is essential to be realistic about what you can accomplish in a given period. Aim big, but it's just as vital to cheer yourself and your team on by accomplishing smaller targets along the road.

Dopamine is released in a burst each time we accomplish one of these objectives, which teaches our brains to seek success and motivates us to move on to the next item on our list.

Setting difficult goals is a key component of success (even if you miss them).

Being in charge of and taking responsibility for our actions increases our motivation to carry them out. Gaining control over your work and allowing your colleagues to do the same can result in an environment that is highly productive.

Celebrate small victories.
Like the majority of business owners, you most likely have ambitious long-term ambitions. But as you are probably aware, lofty goals are rarely achieved overnight.

Instead of waiting to reward yourself only at the finish line, schedule some time each day to give yourself a symbolic fist pump.

"This is a journey — a hard one — and the only way to make it sustainable and enjoyable is to genuinely appreciate your modest wins along the way," said Tech co-founder Frank Gruber.

A daily dose of incentive is provided by celebrating those little victories.

A crucial component of goal-setting and remaining motivated is holding yourself accountable. According to research, 70% of people who gave a weekly update to a buddy after setting a specific goal were successful in completing their accomplishments (reached either halfway or totally), as opposed to the other 30%.

When it comes to giving the much-needed accountability and outlining possible next actions if those objectives are not reached, mentors can be worth their weight in gold. They can offer advice because they've been in your position before.

Bringing everything together

Consider motivation as a way of thinking. The objective you're pursuing doesn't alter, but how you view and approach it does. If necessary, reduce the scope to something you can handle. Then, hold yourself accountable, find a means to manage it yourself (even if it was assigned), and remember to reward yourself when you succeed.

There are many things you may do to get going again even though it can be challenging to get started and begin making noticeable changes when you lack motivation.

Guidelines for Increasing Motivation

The level of motivation and willpower varies for everyone. You may experience moments of intense motivation to accomplish your goals. Other times, you can feel drained or unclear about your goals or the best way to pursue them.

There are actions you may take to help boost your drive if you're lacking it. You can do a variety of things to increase or strengthen your motivation, such as:

To concentrate on things that truly matter to you, change your goals. More than goals based on low-importance objectives, focusing on things that are essential to you will help you get through your obstacles.

Break a task up into smaller, more manageable pieces if it feels too enormous or overwhelming to handle all at once. Then, focus just on completing the first step. For instance, instead of attempting to lose 50 pounds, aim to drop five pounds per week.

Boost your self-assurance. Gaining more self-confidence and skill-confidence will help you achieve your goals because research reveals a link between motivation and confidence.
Remind yourself of your past accomplishments and your areas of strength. This keeps your motivation from being hampered by self-doubt.
Try working on making changes in the areas where you feel insecure so that you feel more capable.

By making something you're not motivated to perform a little more enjoyable, you can improve your mood. When a chore is routinely combined with something enjoyable, you'll feel happier and perhaps even look forward to performing it.
Here are a few instances:

As you run, listen to music.
While you're cleaning the house, give a pal a call and catch up.
Light a scented candle while you're working on your computer.
When you travel for work, rent a luxury automobile.
Ask a friend to join you on your errands.
As you fold laundry, start your favorite TV.
Just be careful that having fun doesn't affect how well you perform. For instance, you can become distracted and work more slowly if you watch TV while writing a paper. Or conversing with a buddy while doing housework could be so distracting that you can't concentrate on what you're doing.

How Therapy Can Aid in Motivating People

You can become more knowledgeable and self-aware, boost your motivation or energy levels, develop coping mechanisms for stressful situations in life, and do all of these things with the aid of therapy. Going to a therapist or counselor can also assist in de-stigmatizing your symptoms and in giving you a sense of validation from someone who can relate to what you're going through.

When a person has low or no motivation, some counseling modalities or specialties may be more helpful than others. Since it encourages you to alter your thought and behavior patterns through strategies like reframing and activity scheduling, cognitive behavioral therapy (CBT) is a well-liked treatment for a lack of motivation. Motivational interviewing (MI), a different choice, is made for those who find it difficult to challenge themselves and feel trapped.

Although there are many different ways to therapy, ultimately what is important is finding the appropriate fit and feeling at ease with your therapist. One of the most crucial factors in assisting you in receiving the benefits of therapy that you require and desire, as well as in feeling safe and accepted in life, is the client-counselor relationship.

Finding your superpower

You advance along your path of purpose when you discover and use your ability.
1. What do you naturally do?

"Your work is placed in your heart when you are born," said Kahlil Gibran

Because our superpowers are so common to us and are taken for granted because we believe everyone else has them, many of us fail to notice their uniqueness.
Your superpowers are the skills you naturally possess.

2. What makes you passionate?
Nelson Mandela once said, "There is no passion to be found in... accepting a life that is less than the one you are capable of living."

Be willing to try to find it. One of the simplest methods to identify your superpower is to take note of what makes you happy—not your parents, instructors, or friends—but YOU.
3. What do you do to make time fly by?

Lao Tau once said, "When I let go of what I am, I become what I might be."

Time seems to vanish, and that's how you know you're using your superpowers. No drugs are required! Whenever I write a song, I isolate myself in my studio and come out many hours later feeling pleased and euphoric with a new melody that seems to have written itself.

4. What distinguishes you as unique or odd?
If you block it, it won't ever exist, according to Martha Graham. "There is a vitality, a life force, a quickening that is translated through you into action, and because there is only one of you in all time, this manifestation is unique."

The key to discovering your superpowers is to own what makes you distinct, even if it appears strange. There is no one else like you. You don't have to attempt to be different. You already are.
Accept your inner freak and you'll find your superpowers.

5. How do your friends seek your advice?
The light that shines from within cannot be dimmed, according to Maya Angelou.

Consider what others approach you for help on. Chances are you have a skill or talent you take for granted but your friends love it. You're an expert at something; you may just not know what it is yet.

6)What activities did you like as a child?
Pablo Picasso famously said, "Every child is an artist; the challenge is how to stay an artist as we get older."

Our superpowers reveal themselves to us as children, adolescents, and young adults, but frequently we lose sight of them in later life because our parents and teachers ignore, downplay, or even attack our authentic natures. According to Brené Brown, 42% of children have shamed away from pursuing some form of creative expression in school.

8)What would you do if money were no object?
Bob Dylan once said, "He who isn't busy dying is busy being born."

What would you do if you didn't have to worry about money?

Find the response that pops up most frequently when answering these questions, and that, my friend, is your superpower.

A combination of skills and interests may make up your powers if you see more than one recurring theme.

You might not always be the one in the room with the best intellect, talent, and creativity. However, you may use these three superpowers to your advantage and still succeed in both your professional and personal lives.

Simply put, you must be:
Persistent
Consistent
Resistant

Not only generally persistent, reliable, and resistant. You must display each at heroic levels. The good news is that anyone can accomplish this goal if they have the same level of determination and ambition to do it.
Just obstinate tenacity and a refusal to quit or yield.

It's not a rare mystical superpower that only a select few possess. This is doable by everyone! Anyone determined and persistent enough can set their sights on anything and work toward making it happen.

"Persistence is the only quality in this world that matters. Nothing is more prevalent than talented men who fail in their endeavors. Genius won't do it; unappreciated genius is practically a proverb. Education won't help because there are many educated misfits in the world. Only tenacity and willpower possess omnipotence. – Calvin Coolidge

"Excellence is an art that is acquired through practice and habit. We don't have virtue or greatness because we act well; rather, we have such things because we have behaved rightly.
We become what we consistently do. Therefore, excellence is a habit rather than an act. ", said Aristotle

Being resilient
Whoever tells you what you can and cannot do with your life should be rejected. They are unaware of the passion and determination you possess. If you persist, they won't fully comprehend what you are capable of. They are not required to lead your life. It's just you.

Don't let other people define you. You establish who you are. – Ginni Rometty

Use your superpowers

You undoubtedly possess a ton of talent, expertise, knowledge, and experience. In their unique manner, everyone does. But if you're not the best at everything, don't stress.

Be tenacious, constant, and resolute. All of us have access to those superpowers. Your natural talent has its limits. The Big Three, though, will get you there in the end.

Everybody experiences problems with motivation from time to time. But what matters is how you handle your lack of motivation. Be gentle to yourself, experiment with methods to boost your motivation, and request assistance if you require it.

There is probably an underlying cause for your burnout that has to be addressed to get your motivation back. By being clear about what that is, you can stop attempting to solve everything in your life and instead concentrate on the one or two things that are truly the cause of everything feeling so difficult.

When you're completely burned out, it's likely to have a bad impact on some aspects of your life, making it difficult to pinpoint the main reason why you're currently having difficulties.
It doesn't matter if it's a real person or a passion—you need to keep in mind your "why."

Your true love and getting back to becoming the person who can support that worthy cause should be the only focus of your efforts.

Knowing true love is what guides you. When you're feeling down or uninspired, thinking back on the people or things that make you who you are provides you the sense of direction you need to keep going even when you feel like you have no more to give.

We must always keep in mind that we are the protagonist of our own stories if anything is to change in our lives. No matter what happens, we are solely accountable for how we react.
The ultimate display of power occasionally involves showing weakness.

You are the hero and a fellow being. None of us can and shouldn't attempt to complete this task alone.

It's crucial to ask for assistance when you're burnt out and look for a support network so you can navigate your way back to yourself.
Freedom for you begins right now.

The secrets to keeping long-term motivation.
One of the keys to keeping long-term motivation is to work on things that follow the Goldilocks Rule. If you find yourself lacking the motivation to do a task, it's likely because it's become tedious or has been placed in a challenging area.

You must figure out a way to push your tasks back to the point where you feel capable but challenged.
According to the Goldilocks Rule, people are most motivated when working on things that are just outside of their current capacity. not that difficult, not too simple. Exactly right.

Only when problems fall within the ideal range of difficulty do people love them. Boring tasks are those that are far beyond your current capabilities.

It is demoralizing to attempt tasks that are clearly beyond your current capabilities. But our brains are immensely motivated by jobs that are on the cusp of success or failure. Nothing is more important to us than learning a skill that is just out of reach right now.

No one owes you anything, but you owe yourself everything.

"No one owes you anything."

Let it sink in as you read it carefully.

The main point is that those who believe life owes them something are being rejected by it.
By their views, the government, their employment, and social conventions. The issue is with you if you aren't wealthy, content, healthy, or fulfilled.

Although it may come out as haughty and unpleasant, the statement is true.
Never-achievers place the blame on others and fail to see their shortcomings.
If you get defensive after reading the last statement, take a step back and look at yourself; perhaps you have been blaming other people for your life the entire time.

Some life isn't fair truths

Not every time can you get what you want.

Absolutely nothing you didn't earn belongs to you.

Stop thinking like a victim, please.

Instead of blaming life and other people for all the things you haven't accomplished, take some personal responsibility.

We don't need to hear your illogical justifications. Even if you believe your ridiculous justifications to be true, YOU don't need to hear them.

You have been harmed more than anyone else by all of those "poor me" justifications because they all amount to DENIAL.

You can begin to construct your happiness once you accept the reality that the world owes you nothing.

When you admit, accept, and comprehend that whatever you DO have in life has to be earned, it is a GIFT to yourself.

Step forward right now and be ready to establish your claim because it is also a show of maturity.

Not just kids develop a sense of entitlement as they get older.
Adults who act as though the world owes them anything and walk around with an inflated ego are just as common.

I don't know what it will take to bring them down from their perch, and perhaps there is a risk that they will remain there indefinitely, looking down on everyone else for the rest of their lives with nothing we can do to change it.

But it's all right.
You don't have to live your life, and you don't have to be concerned about your mistakes.

You are on the correct track as long as YOU understand that feeling entitled brings you nothing but suffering.

We constantly look for these big, great gestures that make us feel like we're going to be promoted, given a ton of money, or told we look fit everywhere we turn. Instead, it might be simpler to simply do what you want to do to make yourself happy, whether it's out of goodwill for others or just because you want to. These are minute-by-minute choices to be better than you were, and improving our ability to be joyful is a habitual process.

When we can presume that no one will assist us, we begin to assist ourselves.
In reality, we are capable of completing tasks on our own without the *expected assistance of others. That very expectation can result in a lifetime of entitlement, softening (in every meaning of the word), and grumbling about how no one is helping out or will give in because it sounds whiny.

Relationships are equal-sided. You owe your part (which should be provided with 100% effort), and they owe theirs. They are responsible if they don't meet you halfway. Nothing more is owed to you by your parents. Whether it was good or bad, anything they did to bring you even close to where you are today shaped you, and it doesn't need to go any further.
Your spouse doesn't owe you dinner after a long day, your boss doesn't pat you on the back, and your buddy doesn't owe you a "happy birthday" on your "big" day.

However, how GRATEFUL do you feel when someone goes out of their way to help you feel good or make your life simpler when it happens?

1: You should be more grateful than you expect to be.

2: Avoid personalizing everything.

The actions of others are not a result of you. What other people say and do is a reflection of their worldviews and aspirations. You won't endure unneeded suffering if you have a strong immune system that protects you from other people's decisions and actions.

3. Don't Assume Anything

No one owes you anything, for example.

"Be as explicit as you can while communicating with others to prevent misunderstandings, grief, and drama" (including with yourself). You have the power to dramatically change your life with this one agreement.

Great if we get some assistance. Not to worry if neither success nor failure is assumed. Nobody owes us any assistance or compensation. This is the attitude you have on your best day ever, every day. It falls on you.

We pass the baton because being powerless makes things simpler. We resist altering because it would be our fault if we failed.
There are no justifications that can shield you from the fact of who you are.

Get rid of the notion that you "deserve" anything, including success, love, and freedom. Begin by BECOMING the person who produces it internally.
Because it's nearly difficult to change others, change yourself.

The crucial insight here is that this is for you. This is a strong message that you should comprehend for yourself. The point is not that you have no obligations to anyone.
For whatever advantages we have gotten from other people, we owe them our thanks and respect.

When you live your life without thinking that anyone owes you anything, you will experience greater success and satisfaction.

And this immediately relates to what we do.

You owe no one a defined career path.

Nobody owes you a clear role.

Your closed sale is not owed to anyone.

You owe no one any political favors.

You owe no one a work-life balance.

Nobody owes you courtesy

Nobody owes you a pay increase.

Nobody owes you a place at the executive table.

You owe nothing to anyone.

Each of these must be earned and obtained by you. You're in charge of running your own life. Until you know the fundamental truth—that you may choose the life you want—this may feel confining.

Great power entails enormous responsibility. Many people have lost sight of this fact or have never even considered it. No one owes you anything because with that power comes accountability.

The sooner you accept your smallness and the fact that no one owes you anything, the more empowered you will feel to shape your destiny.

When you realize that no one owes you anything following your victory or defeat, you stop whining, wishing for the best, become more appreciative of the good things that happen, learn from the bad things that happen, and become more resilient.

They don't have to feed you, pay for your tuition, or give you a free place to stay when you screw up just because they are your parents. They are wonderful parents, and yes, that is usual, but they have no obligation to you. Despite what society would have you believe, they don't.

Another factor is that, regardless of the work you have, you always want to make more money, take more vacation days, receive benefits, etc. Again, that's not something your job owes you. Even if you believe your employer is underpaying you, they owe you nothing.

Become Responsive

Your life is your responsibility. How content or healthy you are, how much money you make, how much freedom you have, and how much respect you have for and receive from others. Everything is owed to you. It was your choice to take the job, so if it's bad, it's your fault. It's not other people's fault that you have unhappy relationships; rather, it's your fault for allowing people with low standards, a bad attitude, and a limited perspective to run your life. It's all up to you.

Your life is your responsibility. You are wasting your time if you are waiting for someone to come and save you, fix you, or even just aid you.

"The only person who can change your life is you." (Oprah Winfrey)

You must genuinely begin to believe in who you are and what you want to accomplish. I might not believe in you, and most likely neither would your friends or perhaps even your parents. To see several methods to accomplish it, you must first persuade yourself and truly believe it.

The Best Ways to Motivate Others and Yourself

Although it seems like we all know how to live well, few of us have the willpower to practice it.
When put to the test using objective factual data, many recommended incentive tactics frequently fall short and show to be useless.

We might be able to develop plans and suggestions for inspiring both ourselves and other people. Sadly, it rarely pays to do what is simple to accomplish.

Techniques for Motivation

Imagine being tasked with inspiring your staff to work harder and more creatively. You may start by thinking about providing alluring rewards.

Although this looks like a workable approach, these incentives are rarely successful and may even cause serious harm, undermining the very motivation you wanted to encourage.

When studying motivation, researchers frequently reach two conclusions:

Not every effort we make to inspire others or ourselves is successful.
In real life, the most successful course of action is rarely the easiest.

Motivation researchers frequently have to start over when it comes to devising successful interventions and motivational supports since the general finding is that what is easy to perform is rarely what is effective.

According to his current moral state, looking forward to something permanent and moving forward toward an even better future is the most consoling outlook a man can have.
Similar conclusions are reached by a lot of people who need to use motivational tactics in their business and personal lives.

When teachers take the effort to adapt the lesson plan into activities that youngsters find engaging, curious-sparking, and personally inspiring, they tend to have considerably better success encouraging their kids to read.

When leaders adopt the employees' perspective and invite them to create their own self-endorsed work goals, they have considerably better success inspiring their team members' inventiveness and diligence.

Even parents who make an effort to genuinely understand their children's reasons for not wanting to be prosocial and take the time to explain the advantages of partaking in such activities are more effective in persuading them to do so.

We frequently discover that we are more successful in motivating others when we forgo giving instructions and commands in favor of working diligently and patiently to understand the situation from the viewpoint of the other party, solicit input from those parties, and then combine all of that data to offer some helpful goals and strategies.

All of these strategies for inspiring and involving people are challenging, but the work is worth it.

Explaining motivation is a difficult task, and understanding it completely is much harder. According to the study of motivation, motives are internal experiences that can be divided into wants, cognitions, and emotions and are influenced by antecedent circumstances such as social contexts and environmental events.

Suggestions for Maintaining Motivation

Finding motivation alone is insufficient. We require rituals, repetition, and reminders to effect long-lasting change.

Reminders

Reminders aid in keeping us focused on a certain commitment. These environmental cues might be easy and basic or intricate and inventive. Here are some recommendations:

1)Just like you would for a client meeting, enter the times for your workout in your planner.
2)Put a picture of the person who inspires you the most to get out of bed and into your running shoes on the wall or as your screensaver.
3)Leave your jogging shoes near your bed to practically trip over your reminders.
4)Choose a song or statement that you find particularly energizing and set your alarm clock to play it.

Repetition
Reminders at regular intervals can encourage repetition, which is necessary for long-lasting change. No matter how challenging it may be, if you simply exercise for the first week or two of the year, it probably falls far short of your expectations. You reach the promised land of change—the cultivation of rituals—through reminders combined with repetition.

Use technology to continually remind your subconscious mind of the world you wish to create. We now have a wide range of fantastic tools thanks to technology.

Schedule the change and set up regular appointments or notifications. Schedule it and have everything ready, whether it's gym time, meal prep time, or bedtime, to make it more likely to occur. The subconscious can more easily adopt the new behavior thanks to these external supports.
Track your progress on a chart that is prominently displayed or use an app that asks you to record your accomplishments; positive feedback boosts motivation.
Plan for when problems arise by creating if-then scenarios.

While jogging, exercising, or doing household chores, listen to audio affirmations.

All day, repeat to yourself subliminal audio and video recordings.
Affirmations can be played to you using software that flashes them on your computer screen surreptitiously.

Rituals as a result of enough repetition and reminders, our brain develops new neural pathways connected to a particular behavior, leading to the formation of rituals. After a month or two, acting in a given way at a certain time gets simpler.
As you establish rituals, repeat them, and generate reminders.

Your inaction is probably the result of neural overload. Small victories and slow progress are the results of modest hopes and aspirations.
Remember that success on the fifth or sixth try is far more likely if you fail and succeed again.

Public pledges have considerable power. Say or write out what you intend to do to yourself, a trusted friend, or a professional. Find someone who can hold you accountable instead.

Another method of verbally stating your desired condition is through affirmations. It gives the brain a strong message that aids in reinforcing the desired changes. Repeating affirmations in the present tense is advised.

Writing down your goals, emotions, and impressions in a journal also strengthens your brain's neural connections and can help you be more persistent.

We improve the likelihood of forming a new habit and replacing less desirable behaviors when we develop practical reminders and repeat them frequently enough to establish rituals.

When motivational treatments concentrate on bolstering people's motivation and mood rather than attempting to improve a particular outcome, such as performance, productivity, achievement, or welfare, they are more effective.

Realistic tools for motivation

1. Engage with your values.
The greatest kept secret is this. You can alter the game if you can, even in minor ways, link the task you do to your principles.

2. Locate your WHY.
Come up with an intriguing goal. Make this into a punch line.

3. Modify your WHY.
There are occasions when you act incorrectly. Are you working on that task to complete it or to gain new knowledge? Just changing your motivation might ignite your fire.

4. Modify your HOW.
By focusing on completing your work well rather than just doing it, you will find that your chores become more pleasurable right away.
It's like perfecting your craft, in my opinion. Make it creative.

Slower is preferable sometimes. Other times, the secret is to turn it into a game and accelerate it. You can set time restrictions and compete with the clock. You can break out of ruts and discover fresh methods to escape the ordinary by altering your approach.

5. Recall the sensation.
One of the quickest methods to alter your mood is to play back scenes and movies in your thoughts. Feeling happy makes it easier to stay motivated.

6. Change to the past, present, or future.
Now and then, you must be present. The right here, right now, isn't always the best. The appeal of changing the tense is that it allows you to reflect on a more delightful past or imagine a more interesting future.

At the same time, if you notice yourself ruminating on a difficult memory, return to the present and revel in the happiness of the moment.
With experience, your temporal abilities will advance.

7. Find a profound metaphor.
Look for a metaphor that inspires you.
Finding a metaphor that links to your ideals is the most effective thing you can do.

8. Make a move.
Motivation frequently comes after action, a secret that, if you know it, will alter your entire existence. Your motivation simply begins to flow as you begin an activity.

9. Link it to positive emotions.
Find a way to connect objects with positive emotions. Play your favorite song while engaging in unpleasant activities, for instance.

It must be a song that elevates your mood enough to block out the discomfort of the work. It's challenging to convince yourself that something is unpleasant when it feels so lovely.

The theme tune is a similar strategy.

10. Make a good first impression.

Most known successful individuals link their interests to their profession and don't rely on others to set the bar. Their internal bar turns into their motivation.

11. You risk losing motivation if you convince yourself that you "HAVE" to do something, "MUST" do something, or "SHOULD" do something.

The ability to choose and simply change your language to "CHOOSE" can be immensely empowering and provide you with the inspiration you need. Make the most of your words by carefully selecting them.

12. Team up.
An unpleasant task is an enjoyable task for one person. Pair up with someone who can help you get over obstacles or who has a skill that compliments yours.

13. Modify your inquiry.
You occasionally need to shift your attention. Change the question to redirect your attention.

Naturally, if you consider what is wrong with this circumstance, you will come up with complaints. You can uncover the positives and get into your groove quickly if you ask yourself what is right about the circumstance.

14. Set aside time for eating, sleeping, and exercising.
When you don't give your body or emotions a break or the proper nourishment, they may start to work against you.

Finding a routine that works for you for eating, sleeping, and moving around or exercising is one easy way to improve the outcomes here.

15. Utilize your advantages.
You become exhausted if you dwell on your inadequacies for too long. You may re energize yourself and find your flow by investing more time in your areas of strength.

You can develop at your best when you focus on your strengths. Find activities that you can do all day long and that you truly enjoy, and seize every opportunity to do more of them. Success reinforces itself, which gives you a boost in momentum.

Test out various motivational strategies to determine what works best for you.

All effective human motivation ultimately boils down to self-motivation, and increasing your self-awareness helps you become more motivated. Learn how to activate your buttons from within.

Self-motivation strategies

1. Schedule your objective.
Creating some external motivation, such as a target date, is one approach to increasing your internal motivation. Put whatever it is that you want to achieve on the calendar. There may be a deadline built into the goal you are pursuing. Examples include studying for an exam or enrolling in a course that has a set completion date.

If your objective is lacking this framework, you can give it one by choosing a deadline by which you could reasonably expect to fulfill it.
Setting a deadline not only keeps you motivated but also allows you to track your progress so that you always know how far you still have to go. This could significantly affect how well you do.

Set a reasonable target date, but repress the impulse to allow more time than you'll need. According to studies, we can mistakenly think that longer goals are more difficult than they are.

Increased procrastination or quitting may result from this.

2. Establish a routine for pursuing your goal.
When you develop the practice of working toward your objective, you no longer need to rely heavily on your motivation.
This can be achieved by allowing your behavior towards the goal to become a habit. Some ways to turn a behavior into a habit include:

a)Choose a trigger.
To act as a trigger for the behavior you want to develop into a habit, pick something you already do every day, such as brushing your teeth or having breakfast.
Making this strategy and putting it in writing might make it more likely to be carried out

b)Begin modestly.
On days when motivation is low, getting started is frequently the most difficult aspect. Starting a modest job, such as five minutes of study or putting on your workout clothing, makes getting started much simpler.

According to The Science of Self Help, these seemingly insignificant tasks can prepare your mind for the activity at hand so the followthrough—a longer study session or a thorough workout—can happen more effortlessly with less mental resistance.

Goal-setting, happiness, personality development, personal development, communication, negotiation, and deception are among the skills you'll learn.

c)Be prepared for errors.
It's wonderful to be enthusiastic and sure that you can accomplish your goal, but it's also easy to be overly optimistic. Every day won't go exactly how you expect it to, and that's okay. Life takes place.

Simply making plans for bad days can help you stay motivated when they occur. Make a note of the potential obstacles as you consider your objective.

Although we can't anticipate every possibility, we can anticipate the challenges that are most likely to arise occasionally in light of our particular situation.

Make a strategy on how to overcome the challenge after you have your list. Now that you have a strategy in place, you can maintain the momentum when that challenge presents itself rather than becoming discouraged and losing motivation.

4. To gain momentum, establish modest goals.
"Make your bed first if you want to change the world. Making your bed in the morning will complete the first task for the day. You'll feel a tiny bit of pride from completing it, which will motivate you to complete further tasks.

Numerous minor victories over time can create a sense of momentum that can ultimately fuel long-term success, especially early in the process, according to research. Start by dividing your major objective into more manageable pieces.

A major objective might be finding new employment. Smaller objectives can include updating your résumé, creating a website for your portfolio, receiving a certification, or going to a networking event.

A new week, month, or year can naturally inspire more motivation when goals are set. We often create mental distance from any perceived inadequacies in our past by psychologically associating these temporal milestones with fresh starts. That is what we mean when we say a motivational Monday.

5. Follow your development.
Observing development can be quite inspiring. There are various tools available to help you keep track of your objectives. This might be as simple as a calendar or to-do list that you can mark off days or items as you finish them.

You might also choose a free application like Trello, which enables you to design a customized digital task board to break down your main goal into smaller ones on a daily, weekly, monthly, or even yearly basis.

6. Give yourself rewards for both small and great accomplishments.
Receiving recognition for our efforts feels fantastic. Rewards, however, can also raise motivation and productivity. Your interest and happiness in your work may increase if you treat yourself to achieving both small and major milestones.

These incentives don't have to be substantial or expensive.
Here is a short list of suggestions for self-care rewards:

i)Take a brief rest
ii)Take a stroll outside.
iii)Savor your preferred snack.
iv)Read a section of your preferred book.
v)Spend some time in meditation.
vi)Stream an episode of your preferred podcast.
vii)Make plans to go out with friends.
viii)Play a game online
ix)Visit a free attraction or museum
x)Take a long shower or bath.
xi)Make a call to a friend or relative.

Prepare yourself to celebrate your accomplishments, both big and small, by taking a few minutes to create your reward list.

7. Accept constructive peer pressure.
In the end, it's you who works hard to accomplish your goals. But the motivation of others can be very powerful.

Even while working alone, research demonstrates that having a sense of belonging to a team can increase perseverance, engagement, and performance. This might entail joining a study group, running team, fitness class, professional organization, or online challenge, depending on your goal.

Another study contends that discussing your objective with someone whose judgment you value can increase your motivation to achieve it. Think about discussing your professional goals with a mentor or manager.

You might decide to discuss your educational objectives with a professor or academic advisor, or your fitness objectives with a motivating coach or fellow gym goer.

8. Demonstrate gratitude (including for yourself).
It could appear that being grateful would result in complacency and acceptance of the status quo. But several investigations have indicated the opposite. Gratitude feelings can:

a)Encourage personal development.

b)Make us feel a member of the group and connected to others

c)Improve motivation for the long term, outside of the time spent practicing appreciation

d)Encourage a desire to contribute

e)Enhance sleep, as well as one's physical and mental well-being

There are several ways to promote a grateful mindset. When you first wake up, take five minutes to list all the things for which you are thankful. Even better, record them in a notebook of thankfulness. Is there a person in your life for whom you are grateful? Send a letter of gratitude to them.

9. Improve your mood.
Positive emotions have been associated with improved work quality and quantity as well as higher levels of productivity. This does not imply that you must always be upbeat because such is unattainable. But if you're not motivated to work toward your objective, a fast mood boost can be all you need.

10. Alter your surroundings.
A change of location occasionally can help you approach your task with a new perspective (and a new sense of motivation). The novelty effect is a transient boost that results from changing your surroundings.

If you often study at home, consider spending some time in the library. Do you regularly use your computer to watch lectures? To watch them while outside in the park, try downloading them to your phone. Try a new workout or change up your jogging route.

11. Keep in mind your "why."
Why is this objective significant to you? Why does that factor matter to you? Why do you think that's important? Keep looking until you find your

ultimate "why"—the principle that motivates your objective.
Set an alarm every morning to remind yourself to take one or two minutes to imagine achievement to further strengthen your "why." How would it feel to succeed in your mission?

Ways to Motivate Yourself Effortlessly

1. Just get going, and then wait for your motivation to come.
You can start right now without waiting for inspiration. Sometimes you just have to start working if you want to be productive every day.

And the strange thing is that when I put in some time working, things start to feel easier and more enjoyable, and my motivation starts to return.

2. If going big makes you procrastinate, start small.
Don't let a project or task's size and difficulty cause you to put it off or put it off indefinitely.

Instead, divide it into manageable pieces, like just putting up your blog or cleaning for five minutes, and then start with one of them.

3. If even a small step still causes you to procrastinate, start small.
Go even smaller if breaking things down and taking a little step still causes you to procrastinate. Just move forward for a minute or two. I'm done now.

Because starting quickly and moving forward with momentum is what matters most.

4. Limit the daily interruptions.
It is difficult to focus when there are distractions readily available all around you.

So close your office door. Away from your workspace or home, switch your smartphone to silent mode. Additionally, utilize a browser extension like StayFocusd to help you stay on task.

5. Encourage the people in your life to hold you accountable.
Inform your pals of what you plan to do on social media, over the phone, or in person. Ask one or more of them to follow up with you and your development frequently.

You'll be much less likely to try to get out of things or quit up at the first hurdle if you do this.

6. Encouragement can be found in the people in your life.
Spend less time with pessimistic folks who are perpetually pessimistic or indifferent.

Spend more of the time you have now freed up with people who are motivated or excited and allow their enthusiasm to rub off on you.

7. Find your inspiration from strangers.
Don't restrict yourself to seeking inspiration only from those closest to you.

You may find a ton of inspiring sayings, books, podcasts, blogs, and success stories online to boost or rejuvenate your motivation.

8. Play upbeat music to keep you motivated.
Playing happy music that encourages me in some manner is one of the easiest things I can do when I'm lacking in energy or motivation.

It usually works great to take a break and listen to a few songs or to work while doing so.

9. Embrace positivity.
Being pessimistic can sap your will and vitality.

On the other hand, a constructive and upbeat perspective can reinvigorate and restore your motivation.

Therefore, when you seem to be in a bad circumstance, ask yourself these questions.

What is one positive aspect of this? And what is this place's untapped opportunity?

10. When you falter, be kind to yourself.
When you slip or fail, it's so simple to fall into the trap of punishing yourself.

But in my experience, that doesn't work that well. Simply put, you feel worse and less inspired.

Try this instead the next time: be polite to yourself, gently prod yourself back onto the road you were on, and move ahead one small step.

11. Think positively about your mistakes.
Be proactive with your setbacks to make them more valuable and less painful. When you fall, think to yourself:

What one lesson can I draw from this failure?

Then, keep that lesson in mind and put it into practice to make your work better.

12. To gauge your progress, look at how you compare to yourself.
Instead of letting comparisons to those who are so far ahead of you sap your confidence and enthusiasm.

13. Fair competition is encouraged.
Make a fun competition out of doing a tedious or routine chore first with a friend when you're at work or in school. Even that small amount of rivalry tends to keep things interesting.

For added incentive, you can even include a small gift, such as the winner receiving a free ice cream cone or drink from the other person.

14. Remind yourself of the purpose behind your efforts.
It's simple to lose track of your motivations and energy levels when undertaking a task.

Take two minutes to list your top three motivations for working at this job, pursuing an education, exercising, saving money, or doing something else.

Put your note somewhere you'll see it every day or save it to your phone so you can find it quickly when you need a boost of motivation.

15. Remind yourself of the things you are eschewing.
Another way to spur yourself on is to consider the consequences of continuing along your current route.

Think about it:

What will happen if I stay on this course for another year? And if so, for an additional six years?

16. Be appreciative of what you have.
It's simple to begin viewing your life and its elements through a negative lens when motivation is low.

Asking yourself a question like this will help you focus on what you still have and who you are while regaining positivity and motivation.

17. Change things up.
A rut will sap your motivation. So test different plans. Make a task into a competition, either with yourself or another person.

Instead of just going through the motions, mix up your workout routine. Listen to podcasts and music you don't typically listen to.

To maintain motivation, it's usually best to provide new information and variety (or to recharge it).

18. Organize your work area.
Spend a few seconds tidying it up.
Having a clean, minimalist desk makes it easier to think clearly, and it makes you feel more

concentrated and prepared to take on the next assignment (or small step).

19. Just have one thing on your list of things to do.
A lengthy to-do list can seriously undermine motivation.

In that case, try condensing your present to-do list to a single item. The one you've been putting off for far too long, or possibly the one that's currently most important to you.

Then begin by taking a step, no matter how big, small, or tiny.

Additionally, have a separate list of upcoming jobs hidden someplace where you can't see it.

20. Remind yourself to take breaks.
Few things can sap everyday motivation as quickly as nonstop work.
Instead, work for 45 minutes every hour and then take a break to eat a snack, go outside for some fresh air, or stretch for a few minutes.

Your energy, focus, and motivation will simply last longer, which will allow you to accomplish more in a day and a week and produce work of a higher caliber.

21. Adjust the size of your target.
Set a modest goal to help you rediscover your motivation if a larger goal in your life becomes overwhelming.
And if a modest goal doesn't seem motivated, try raising the bar with a bigger objective and observe how it changes your level of drive.

22. Exercise.
Exercise has effects beyond the physical body. Just 20 to 30 minutes of aerobics can help you feel more relaxed and focused.

23. Spend two minutes reflecting on your accomplishments.
Close your eyes and allow the best moments of your life, regardless of the area in which they occurred, to flow over you. Make use of those motivation-boosting memories.

24. Celebrate your achievements and give yourself rewards.
Your motivation is likely to increase if you're anticipating a pleasant reward that you'll receive yourself once a work or project is completed.

It's also common for motivation and positivity to be refueled if you celebrate an accomplishment in another way, such as by taking a minute to appreciate what you accomplished or by telling someone about it.

So celebrate and dangle those goodies to keep yourself motivated.

25. Before you begin, do some study.
You can avoid hazards by getting advice from those who have already been where you want to go and have done what you want to accomplish. And to provide you with a reasonable success timeline.

This is crucial to remember when things aren't moving along as quickly as you'd want.

26. Take a two-minute meditation break,
Sit down with your eyes closed and concentrate just on your breathing for two minutes.
This relaxes and relieves tension within.

Conclusion

It can be difficult to become motivated, and it can be even harder to stay motivated.
Set reasonable goals that inspire you instead of goals that will drain your energy.
Remind yourself of the incentive you are looking for to complete tasks.
Keep in mind the compromise you must make to achieve your goals, then give it your all.
Eliminate the things that distract you and then focus on one item to attain your goals.

By listing three things for which you are thankful, you can boost your mood.
Declutter and arrange your surroundings to help yourself stay motivated. A tidy space equals a tidy mind.

Realize your full potential; you are stronger than you realize.

Just get started and wait for the motivation to come.

Popular Motivation Quotes to Boost Your Drive

The next time you're lacking motivation, go through these sayings and phrases.

"Failure only occurs when you fall and remain down."
-Aberjhani

"Always go for the present above the past. What shall we now do? ”
-Daniel Tracy

"You are your boss. The master keys to the inner locks are only in your possession."
-Atul Ray

"Have faith in yourself! Have confidence in your skills! You cannot be successful or happy without a modest but acceptable trust in your abilities."
-Peale, Norman Vincent

"If you can imagine it, you can achieve it."
-Mickey Disney

"There is a way where there is a will. If there is even a remote possibility that you can prevent what you desire from happening, do it. Pry open the door, or if necessary, shove your foot inside to keep it open."
-Pamela Kael

"Start where you are and work with whatever tools you may have at your disposal; better tools will be found as you go along. Do not wait; the time will never be 'just right."
-Herbert George

"Go on ahead. Keep moving forward and don't stop or pause; instead, aim for the goal in front of you."
-Paul Whitefield

"Those who trust in the beauty of their dreams have the future in their hands."
-Franklin D. Roosevelt

"Target the moon. You might hit a star if you miss."
-W. Claude Stone

"Don't keep an eye on the time; follow its lead. Move forward."
-Sam Levenson

"There will be challenges. Doubters will exist. Mistakes will be made. However, there are no boundaries when working hard."
-Phelps, Michael

"Keep your feet firmly planted while keeping your gaze on the stars."
-Franklin D. Roosevelt

"To strike the mark, we aim above the mark."
-Theodore Waldo Emerson

"Continually setting higher goals is one approach to maintain momentum."
-Mike Korda

"Modify your life right now. Act immediately and without delay. Don't risk the future."
-De Beauvoir, Simone

You simply cannot defeat someone who never quits up.
-Bear Ruth

"Begin where you're at. Utilize your resources. Work your best."
-Ashe, Arthur

"Why should you keep pursuing your goals? Seeing the expression on the faces of those who told you you couldn't. . . will be inestimable."
-John Ngo

"Never give up because that is precisely the moment and location when the tide will turn."
-Judith Beecher Stow

You cannot satisfy everyone's needs in one way.
You cannot complete everything at once.
You can't perform every task flawlessly.
You cannot perform all tasks as superior to anyone else.
Your humanity, like everyone else's, is becoming apparent.

You need to discover who you are and live up to that.
You must select what comes first and then act accordingly.
You must identify and play to your strengths.

You must learn to stop comparing yourself to others.
Since no one else is competing to be "you,"

You'll have mastered the art of embracing your individuality.
You'll have mastered the ability to decide what to prioritize.
You'll have mastered coping with your constraints.
You will have gained the ability to treat yourself with respect.

No one but you can motivate yourself to live your full life.
Always remember that being who you are is not just your right, but also your job, that life is a gift to be cherished rather than a problem to be solved.
And you'll be able to keep one step ahead of whatever used to depress you.

www.ingramcontent.com/pod-product-compliance
Lightning Source LLC
LaVergne TN
LVHW010608160826
845677LV00013B/3316

* 9 7 9 8 3 5 1 9 6 2 0 5 4 *